THE BOOK OF
MAHJONG
AN ILLUSTRATED GUIDE

麻將

THE BOOK OF MAHJONG

AN ILLUSTRATED GUIDE

Amy Lo

TUTTLE PUBLISHING
BOSTON • RUTLAND, VERMONT • TOKYO

Published by Tuttle Publishing, an imprint of Periplus Editions (HK) Ltd., with editorial offices at 153 Milk Street, Boston, MA 02109 and 130 Joo Seng Road, #06-01/03, Singapore 368357.

LCC Card No. 2002727002
ISBN 0-8048-3302-8

Printed in Singapore

Distribution:

North America, Latin America & Europe
Tuttle Publishing
364 Innovation Drive
North Clarendon, VT 05759-9436
Tel: (802) 773 8930; Fax: (802) 773 6993
Email: info@tuttlepublishing.com
www.tuttlepublishing.com

Japan
Tuttle Publishing
Yaekari Building, 3rd Floor
5-4-12 Osaki, Shinagawa-ku
Tokyo 141 0032
Tel: (03) 5437 0171; Fax: (03) 5437 0755
Email: tuttle-sales@gol.com

Asia Pacific
Berkeley Books Pte. Ltd.
130 Joo Seng Road #06-01/03
Singapore 368357
Tel: (65) 6280 3320; Fax: (65) 6280 6290
Email: inquiries@periplus.com.sg
www.periplus.com

10 09 08 07 06 05
10 9 8 7 6 5

Contents

The Mahjong Game

Mahjong is called "Mahjek," which means "sparrow," by Cantonese players. The derivative of this name is uncertain, but it may have something to do with the sound of the sparrow and the fact that mahjong is such a noisy game. It may also describe the players' arms and how they constantly and quickly move the tiles, looking similar to jumping sparrows. Or it may refer back to the old days when seamen played mahjong at sea and the wind blew the game cards (mahjong was originally played with cards) like a group of sparrows flying away.

For the Chinese, as well as many other Asians, mahjong is a way of life, a favorite pastime that has been fully absorbed into the daily culture. Indeed, in many societies, the typical topic for opening a conversation is talk of weather or sports, but arguably the most prevalent icebreaker in the Chinese community is the previous evening's mahjong score. The game is played at home, in private clubs, and at social occasions—birthdays, wedding banquets, holidays—and is a popular way of entertaining business clients.

Regular mahjong players idolize the game, which has resulted in such rhetoric as mahjong "truthfully expresses one's individuality" or "provides the opportunity to express personal freedom and indulge in self-satisfaction" being commonly heard.

For many, the game offers not only an occasion for socializing, but also, a way to demonstrate one's ability to be one's own boss, without being swayed by adverse comments from opponents.

Despite its captivating appeal, devotees are often at a loss to explain why the game exerts such a hold on them. Some claim that its strategic maneuvers simulate real-life challenges. Once the game starts, players cast all their cares behind them as they immerse themselves totally into a world of expectation and anticipation. The game's seemingly endless variations make it difficult to judge an opponent's strength, thus adding to its intrigue. Since no two games are the same, each presents a unique set of challenges as well as opportunities.

A more immediate reason for the game's popularity is that it is simple to learn and relatively easy to play. Players also claim that it relieves hypertension, subdues repression, and improves mental concentration and alertness. After an exhausting week at work, it is hard to find a better therapy than to sit down with relatives and friends, four to a table, over a sea of tiles. The familiar cries of "Sheung," "Pung," and the victorious "Sik," dispel all cares as this fantasy world is entered.

The history of mahjong has been obscured by time, although it is believed to have evolved from a card game first played a millennium ago. Legend has it that a fisherman devised it to distract his fellow sailors from yearning to return to shore whenever they were hit by rough seas. Many centuries later, the love affair with the game has not only endured but intensified. Today, people from all walks of life take to mahjong as a favorite pastime.

The Cantonese often refer to the game as "mahjek," which means "sparrow," although the origin of the term is uncertain. Maybe it has something to do with the noisy, garbled sounds that the tiles make when they are being shuffled. Another explanation could be that the players are constantly moving the tiles in a manner that mimics hopping sparrows. Yet another view contends that in the old days when sailors played the game at sea, it was likely that the strong breeze would have tossed some cards away, evoking the image of a flock of darting sparrows.

In the last few decades, the migration of Asians to the West has increased dramatically. As a result, mahjong has become more popular in Western societies, a trend that has heightened the need for a good English-language book on the game. It is all the more surprising that very few mahjong books written by Asians have ever been published in English. Even the handful that have are of limited use, since they cover only the Western and Japanese versions of the game, which are not played by, or known to, most Asians.

With this vacuum acknowledged, this book seeks to introduce authentic Chinese mahjong to the English-speaking world. It is believed that this is the first book of mahjong to cover fully the instructions of the original basic 13-tile game, also known as the Cantonese Game and the Old Rules Game. For completeness, the book also includes the most popular variations in Chinese mahjong, the Shanghai Game, the 16-Tile or Taiwanese Game and the 12-Tile Game. It is hoped that this book will seduce new players with the unique appeal and pleasures of the game, thereby keeping the mahjong tradition alive for many generations to come.

THE BOOK OF

MAHJONG

AN ILLUSTRATED GUIDE

CHAPTER ONE

THE GAME OF MAHJONG 麻將

A game of mahjong calls for four players seated at a square table, one on each side. Each player draws a hand of 13 tiles from the center of the table, and the ritual of tile exchange begins. One at a time, the players draw a new tile from the table or pick up a matching tile discarded by another player. At the same time, players discard their unmatched tiles, seeking with each move to create a matched hand.

Thus, the initial objective of each player is to match all the tiles in his or her hand before the other players do. The first player to do so wins the game. The second objective is to assemble the highest-scoring hand at the table. The score, which is based on the probability of achieving a certain combination of tiles, is calculated by totaling the winning points of all the tiles in the hand. In general, the lower the probability of achieving a certain combination, the higher the score awarded. Of course, the converse is true as well.

Mahjong is a game both of chance and risk as there is not one without the other. Yet another factor is time. A higher-scoring hand takes longer to assemble. In other words, the longer you delay putting together your hand, the greater is your risk of losing the game to a player who may beat you to it.

Mahjong is also a game of strategy. You must cultivate a keen eye for the pattern of discards and matching of tiles by your opponents. From this observation, you must try to predict what patterns the other players are likely to be assembling. On the one hand, you try to utilize your opponents' discards to match your tiles, thus maximizing your chance of winning. On the other hand, you try to prevent your opponents from matching their tiles with your discards.

Arguably, the most intriguing part of the game lies in the decision making. You will constantly wonder whether to risk discarding a tile (thus giving your opponents a chance of matching theirs) to increase your chance of assembling a higher-scoring hand, or to hold on to your hand for a safe win, thereby forgoing the opportunity of a better score. Remorse after a hand is common. For some, it is the regret of not having had the boldness to go for a big hand. For others, it is the recklessly ambitious pursuit of a big hand, only to have another player reveal a matched hand first. Most observers believe that a player's behavior reflects his or her true personality.

The magic of mahjong is the feeling of exhilaration that comes from winning a hand as well as from knowing that a wrong move or the loss of a hand can still lead to victory eventually. A player always sees another chance in the next hand. He or she knows that as the game unfolds, many new opportunities will present themselves, along with an endless stream of hopes and expectations, a situation rarely, if ever, encountered in real life.

1.1 The Tiles 牌

Mahjong tiles are small rectangular blocks of plastic, with symbols engraved on the face of each one. In the past, the tiles were made of ivory, animal bone, or bamboo. The sizes vary and can range from approximately 1/2 inch thick by 3/4 inch wide by 1 inch tall to 1 inch thick by 1.5 inches wide by 2 inches tall.

A standard mahjong set contains 136 tiles, divided into two major groups: the Common (or Number) tiles and the Honor tiles. In addition, there are 8 optional Flower tiles, making a total of 144 tiles.

(1) The Common tiles consist of three suits, each composed of four sets of tiles. Each set is numbered one through nine.

The Circle Tiles (Tung Jee) 筒子牌

The Bamboo Tiles (Sok Jee) 索子牌

Note: The No. 1 Bamboo tile is represented by the picture of a sparrow.

The Character Tiles (Man Jee) 萬子牌

(2) The Honor tiles consist of the Dragons and the Winds: (Fan Jee) 番子

There are three Dragons, Red, Green, and White, with four tiles each. 三元牌

Red (Chung), Green (Fat), White (Bak) 中發白

There are four Winds, East, South, West, and North, with four tiles each. 風牌

East (Dong), South (Nam), West (Say), North (Buk)

(3) An optional group of 8 Flower tiles exists: Spring, Summer, Autumn, Winter, Plum, Orchid, Chrysanthemum, and Bamboo (no relationship to the Bamboo tiles in the Common group). (Far Pai) 花牌

1.2 Accessories

◆ Dice 骰子

Dice are used for the allocation of seats, for the designation of the First Dealer, and for breaking the wall of tiles for each game. A set of two or three dice may be used, although beginners are advised to use only two dice for all purposes. This is because the highest sum of dots from three dice is 18, which exceeds the number of tile stacks in each section of the walls, thus complicating the breaking of the walls.

◆ First Dealer Indicator (Hei Jong) 起莊

The indicator is displayed at the left-hand corner of the First Dealer to remind the players to change the Wind in each round of the game.

◆ Dealer and Wind Indicator (Jong) 莊

The Indicator, which is used to designate the Dealer in each hand of the game, can be any one of many different designs. When a hand is finished, the Indicator is passed to the next Dealer. The Indicator is also used to indicate the Wind of the round. Accordingly, the Wind sign shown on the Indicator is also changed after each round.

1.3 A Hand of Tiles 一手牌

A playing hand consists of 13 tiles. A winning hand consists of four matched sets of 3 tiles each and one pair called the Eyes of the hand. A matched set can be a Sequence or a Triplet. Thus, a player is always waiting for either a 14th tile that completes the last matched set or the Eyes to declare a win.

A sequence is composed of any three consecutive numbers of the same suit. (Sun Jee) 順子

A Triplet is composed of any three identical tiles of the same suit.(Hak Jee) 刻子

The Eyes can be any 2 identical tiles.
(Ngan, Jiang) 眼，將

1.4 A Few Examples of Winning Hands

A. Chicken Hand: Consists of Sequences and Triplets of more than one suit. It is the easiest way to assemble a winning hand. 雞糊

B. Common Hand: Consists of only Sequences of more than one suit. 平糊

C. All Triplets Hand: Consists of only Triplets of more than one suit. 對對糊

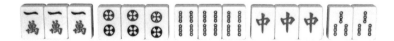

D. Mixed One-Suit Hand: Combines tiles in one suit and Honor tiles. 混一色

E. Pure One-Suit Hand: Consists of tiles in only one suit. 清一色

F. All Honor Tiles Hand: Consists of Honor tiles only. 全字

G. 13-Terminal Tile Hand: Consists of one each of numbers one and nine of each Common suit and one each of the Honor tiles, plus one additional tile that matches any of the tiles in the hand. 十三么

1.5 Players and Their Respective Playing Positions

A game of mahjong requires four players. The players sit around a square table, and the game proceeds in a counterclockwise direction. Each player calls the player on his or her right the Lower House, the player on his or her left the Upper House, and the player sitting across the table the Opposite House.

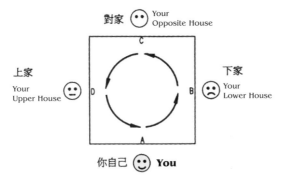

There is a Dealer for each hand of the game. His or her sole function is to commence the game by casting the dice and breaking the walls of tiles.

During each and every hand of the game, the Dealer is called the East House. His or her Lower House is the South House, the Opposite House is the West House, and the Upper House is the North House.

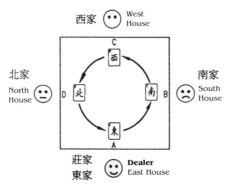

1.6 Playing Directions

The allocation of each player's seat, the designation of the First Dealer, and the playing of the game proceed in a counterclockwise direction. The order in which the players take turns to retrieve a tile and discard a tile also travels counterclockwise. As has been pointed out, each player calls the player on his or her right the Lower House, the player in front of him or her the Opposite House, and the player to the left the Upper House. The breaking of the walls and the drawing of tiles from the wall proceed in a clockwise direction, however.

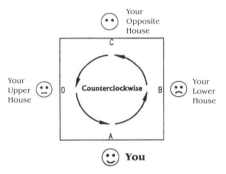

Retrieving and discarding tiles

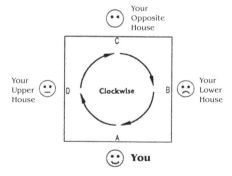

Breaking of the walls and drawing of tiles

1.7 Different Rules of Mahjong Game

It is natural that a game played by many ethnic groups for centuries would have developed variations and even very different sets of rules. Today, the most commonly known rules of play are:

(1) The Old Rules, also known as the 13–tile Cantonese Game 舊章十三張廣東牌
(2) The New Rules, also known as the Shanghai Game 新章 上海牌
(3) The 12-Tile Game 十二張
(4) The 16-Tile Game, also known as the Taiwanese Game 十六張台灣牌

In all of these games, the rules are basically the same. The major difference lies in the method of scoring, which changes according to the many variations in the combinations of tiles and the sets in a winning hand. Minor differences include the method of seat arrangement, the selection of the First Dealer, the construction of the wall, the discarding of tiles, the displaying of the revealed sequence, terminology, and so on.

This book provides instructions for all four versions of the game. The Cantonese Game (Old Rules) is considered the most practical for beginners to learn because of its simpler scoring system. Of the four games, the most complicated is the Shanghai Game, due to its many combinations.

CHAPTER TWO

THE CANTONESE GAME

十三張廣東牌

(The Old Rule 13-Tile Game)

Mahjong is a game of strategy, with one player's personality and behavior often affecting another player's chances of winning. An inexperienced or careless player can inadvertently help an opponent to assemble a high-scoring hand. Mahjong is also a game of luck. Players believe strongly in Feng Shui, a belief that supernatural powers can bring good luck to a person occupying a particular seat at a certain time. For this reason, rightly or wrongly, players can become very finicky about where they sit. Thus, it is not difficult to understand why seat allocation is an important part of the game.

2.1 Seat Allocation (Jup Wai) 執位

Once all four players are seated randomly around a square table, any player may pick out four different Wind tiles and place them face down on the table. After these Wind tiles have been thoroughly mixed, they are stacked up one on top of another.

One player casts a set of two or three dice and the dots are summed. The dice caster counts him- or herself as 1, followed by the player at his or her right as 2, and thus the sequence of counting is carried out counterclockwise until the sum is reached. The player who is the last one to be counted will pick up the top tile on the stack. The player at his or her right picks up the next tile, the opposite player picks up the third, and the player at his or her left picks up the last tile. Whoever picks up the East Wind tile from the stack will have the prerogative of selecting the first seat. The player with the South Wind tile will be seated at the right of the East Wind player and will be the East's Lower House. The player with the West Wind tile will be seated opposite the East Wind player and will be the East's Opposite House. The last player, or the one with the North Wind

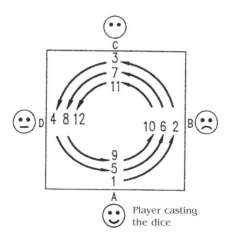

Player casting
the dice

tile, will be seated at the left of the East Wind player, and will be the East's Upper House.

For example, four players occupy seats A, B, C, and D as shown below. The player at side A casts the dice and the total number of dots is 3 (or 7 or 11). The player at side C should pick the top tile from the stack, the player at side D picks the second tile, the player at side A the third. The last tile belongs to the player at side B.

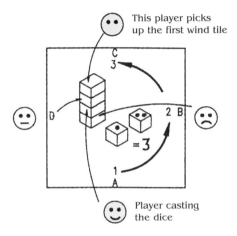

This player picks up the first wind tile

Player casting the dice

If the player with the East Wind tile chooses to sit at side A, then the players with the South Wind tile and the West Wind tile will be seated at side B and side C, respectively. The player with the North Wind tile will be seated at side D.

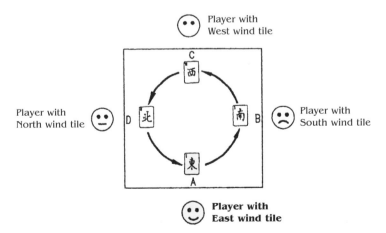

Player with West wind tile

Player with North wind tile

Player with South wind tile

Player with East wind tile

2.2 Building the Walls (Darp Pai) 疊牌

Once everyone is seated in his or her designated seat, all the players take part in turning the tiles face down and mixing them thoroughly. Each player then forms a row of 17 tiles (18 if the Flower tiles are also used in the game; see Section 2.17, page 47), 2 tiles high and face down in front of him- or herself.

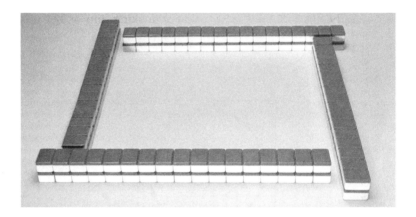

To add sophistication to the game when building the walls, each player first picks up 5 tiles with both hands (6 tiles if playing with the Flower tiles) to make the initial row of tiles. He or she then picks up 3 tiles in each hand and adds them separately to each end of the existing row. The last step is repeated so that the final row consists of 17 tiles. After carefully aligning the tiles against the frame built around the mahjong table, the player makes another row of tiles in the same manner. When this is done, he or she stacks the tiles and pushes the double-deck row toward the center of the table, joining the other rows as connecting walls. Some mahjong sets come with four rulers, each equivalent to the length of 18 tiles. The rulers are useful for gauging the length of the rows and keeping the walls of tiles straight and tidy.

2.3 Designating the First Dealer (Dar Jong) 起莊 打莊

There is a Dealer for each hand of the game. His or her function is to start the game and break the walls. In the ritual of choosing the

First Dealer, the player who picked the East Wind tile during the seat allocation now casts two dice, and the dots are summed. The same player begins to count counterclockwise, making him- or herself 1, the next player 2, and so forth until that sum is reached. The last player counted is named the First Dealer.

Example: The player with the East Wind tile sitting at side A of the table casts the dice and the total number of the dots is five. The counting begins and ends at that player, making him or her the First Dealer.

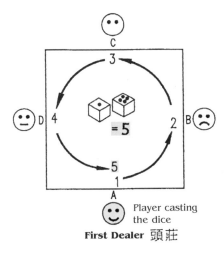

Player casting the dice

First Dealer 頭莊

2.4 Breaking the Walls (Hoi Pai) 開牌

The First Dealer commences the game. Starting at the right side of the wall of tiles he or she is facing, the Dealer counts the stacks clockwise according to the total number of dots on the dice cast, in this case five. The First Dealer then separates the first five stacks from the rest of the wall, so as to mark the breaking point. From the breaking point, the First Dealer picks up 4 tiles from the first 2 stacks (the sixth and seventh stacks) from the walls. He or she is followed by the Lower House, Opposite House, and Upper House. Each player proceeds to pick up two stacks at a time for three turns and a single tile at the fourth turn, thus ending with 13 tiles in his or her playing hand.

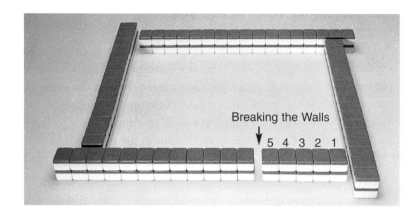

Breaking the Walls

5 4 3 2 1

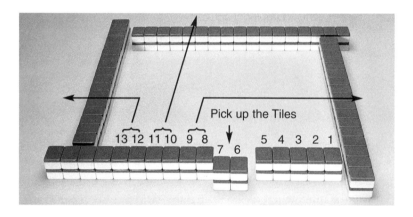

Pick up the Tiles

13 12 11 10 9 8 7 6 5 4 3 2 1

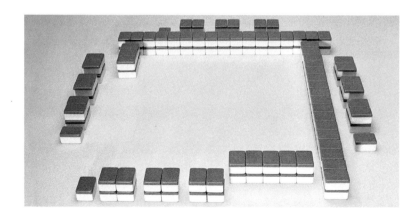

2.4.1 Leaping the Tiles (Til Pai) 跳牌

A little ritual is usually performed by the Dealer after he or she picks up the 12th tile. The Dealer does not have to wait until all three players have picked up their 13th tile to make the first draw. He or she can start the exchange process by picking up a 14th tile from the wall at the same time the 13th tile is picked up (leaping over), to save a little time and to add some sophistication to the game.

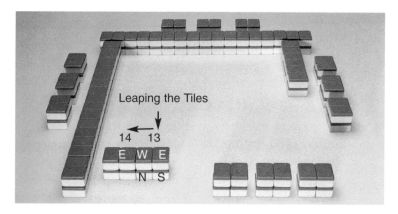

Each player now has 13 tiles (the Dealer has 14 if the leap was included), which he or she arranges in a row facing him- or herself. Beginners benefit by placing all the matched tiles on the left side and all the unmatched tiles on the right. By doing so, a player can easily identify what is in the hand and thus avoid accidentally

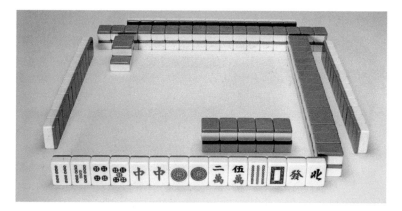

discarding a matching tile. As a courtesy, players always play with their right hands.

2.5 Matching the Tiles (Jo Pai) 做牌

The tiles are matched in an exchange process. The exchange process begins with the Dealer, who discards the first tile from his or her hand of 14. Moving counterclockwise, each player takes a turn drawing a tile from the remaining walls and discarding the least desirable tile from his or her hand. The least desirable tile could well be the one just drawn from the walls. Alternatively, instead of drawing a tile from the walls, a player can claim a tile discarded by another player, that will go toward making a matched set. Thus, a matched set can be assembled by using only the tiles in the playing hand or by claiming a tile discarded by another player. In any case, by retrieving a tile to replace the one immediately discarded, each player always keeps 13 tiles in his playing hand. Through this exchange process, the players try to rid themselves of their undesirable tiles in order to put together a winning hand. The same procedure is continued until one player matches all of the tiles in his or her hand.

In some Chinese mahjong games, not all the tiles on the remaining walls are available for drawing. In the Cantonese Game, there will always be 14 tiles that are untouchable at the tail ends of the walls. In the 16-Tile Game, the number of untouchable tiles is 16. But in the Shanghai Game, every single tile is available for drawing.

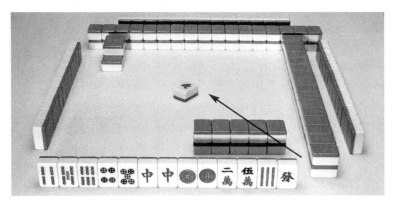

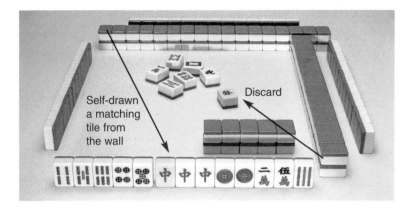

2.6 Claiming a Discarded Tile

2.6.1 Sheung – To Match a Sequence 上牌

When a player holds 2 of the 3 tiles necessary to form a Sequence, he may claim the third matching tile only from his Upper House (that is, the player to the left) by declaring Sheung. By doing so, he or she picks up the matching tile, adding it to the two matching tiles, and then displays the Sequence face up on the table. Of course, the player must also discard a tile to keep the total number of tiles in his or her hand at 13. After that, the player's Lower House continues the game as usual.

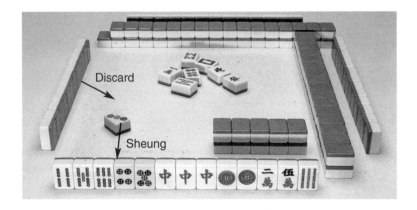

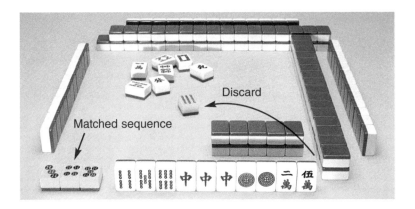

2.6.2 Pung – To Match a Triplet 碰牌

When a player holds a pair of identical tiles, he or she may claim a third matching tile when it is discarded by any of the other three players by declaring Pung. By doing so, he or she picks up the discarded tile, adding it to the two matching tiles, and displays the Triplet face up on the table. The player then discards a tile and the person on the right (his or her Lower House) continues the game as usual. Because the player who declares Pung has higher priority over any player who declares Sheung, he must declare Pung as soon as the matching tile is discarded on the table and before the Lower House of the discarder has had a chance to declare Sheung.

A player who fails to declare Pung cannot claim the same tile discarded by other players until after he or she has made a discard. Of course, all the players must keep track of the recent discards.

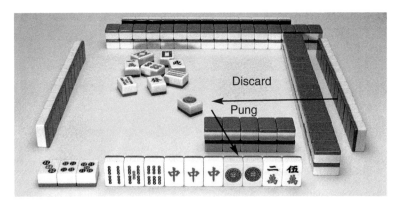

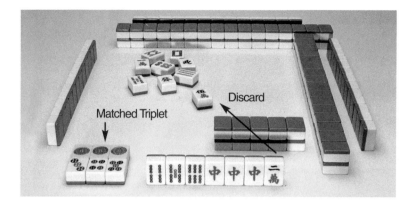

Matched Triplet   Discard

2.6.3 Revealed and Concealed Sets

When a tile that completes a set is taken from a discard, the matched set must be displayed face up on the table. This is called a revealed set.

When a matched set is formed in the first 13 tiles drawn from the wall or is formed with a tile drawn from the wall by the player, the matched set is kept in the hand, unrevealed to the other players. The set is called a concealed set.

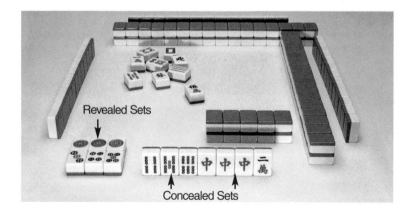

Revealed Sets

Concealed Sets

2.6.4 Gong – To Match a Quadruplet 開槓

A. Drawing the fourth identical tile

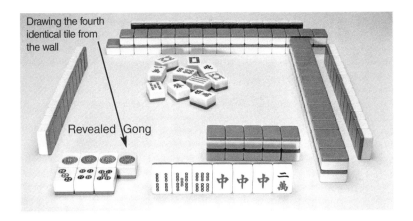

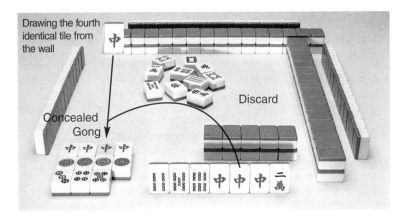

When a player who has a revealed or concealed Triplet draws the fourth identical tile from the wall, he or she has the option of keeping it to match an already-held concealed Sequence or to declare Gong. By declaring Gong, the player adds the drawn tile to the revealed or concealed Triplet and displays the Quadruplet on the table.

B. Claiming the fourth identical tile

It is only when a player has a concealed Triplet that he or she can declare Gong and claim the fourth identical tile discarded by any player. But the Quadruplet must be revealed on the table afterward.

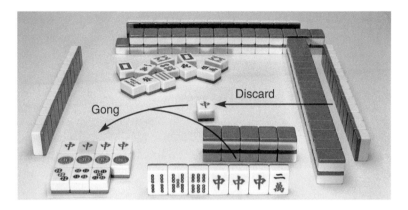

Remember, each time a player declares Gong and adds the fourth identical tile to a Triplet, he or she must immediately draw a makeup tile from the end of the wall and discard a tile. The game is continued by the player's Lower House (Bo Pai).

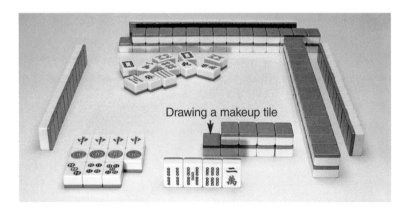

Revealed Gong (Ming Gong) 明槓
Declaring Gong by adding the self-drawn fourth identical tile to a revealed Triplet.

Concealed Gong (Um Gong) 暗槓
Declaring Gong by adding the self-drawn or claimed fourth identical tile to a concealed Triplet.

The purposes of declaring Gong are (1) to disrupt the other players' turns in order to draw a tile from the wall, (2) to prevent other players from claiming the tile, (3) to gain an extra chance to draw a tile, and (4) to gain an additional Fan for a winning hand.

2.6.5 Priority in Claiming Discards

First Priority: To match the last set of the tiles in a winning hand by declaring Sik, one can claim the winning tile discarded by any other player.

Second Priority: To match a Triplet by declaring Pung, or to match a Quadruplet by declaring Gong, one can claim the discard from any other player.

Third Priority: To match a Sequence by declaring Sheung, one can claim the discard only from his or her Upper House (that is, the player to the left).

Example: You have the No. 4 and No. 5 Circle tiles in your playing hand. You are ready to claim the No. 3 Circle tile discarded by your Upper House, to form a Sequence of Nos. 3, 4, and 5. If, however, your Lower or Opposite House is holding a pair of No. 3 Circle Tiles, he or she has higher priority to claim the discard to match a Triplet.

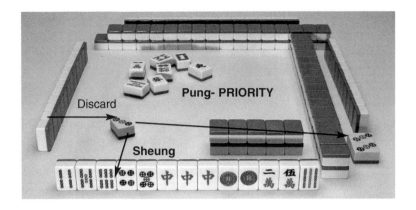

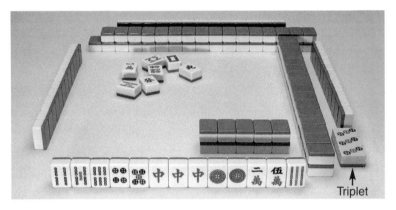

2.7 When to Declare a Win (Ting Pai) 聽牌

Since a winning hand consists of 14 tiles (except when a hand consists of one or more Quadruplets, each of which has an extra tile), when a player matches all the 13 tiles in his or her hand, only one final matching tile is needed to complete the hand.

The 13 matched tiles are called a Ready Hand, and the holder of a Ready Hand is called a Calling Player. The final matching tile is called the Winning Tile.

A Calling Player can complete a hand by drawing the Winning Tile from the walls during his or her turn, or by claiming the Winning Tile when another player discards a tile or declares a revealed Gong. Note that if a player fails to claim the Winning Tile when it is first discarded by a player, he or she cannot claim the

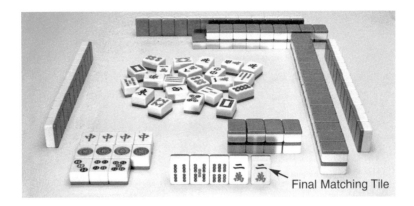

Final Matching Tile

Winning Tile discarded by other players until after making his or her own discard. The player can declare a win, however, if the same Winning Tile is self-drawn. In the 16-Tile Game, a self-drawn tile is treated just like a discarded tile in this situation.

When a player declares a Win, or Sik, he or she must first turn all of his or her tiles face up on the table and then add the Winning Tile to the hand, so as to allow the other players to examine the hand, and to calculate the score. But if the Winning Tile is self-drawn, the winner must first reveal the self-drawn tile before turning all the tiles face up on the table.

When two or more players declare a win by claiming the same discarded tile, the Lower House of the discarder has first priority, while the Upper House has lowest priority. There is only one exception to this: when the holder of a 13 Terminal Tile Hand claims the discarded tile to complete a winning hand, he or she can declare a win regardless of his or her position relative to the tile-discarding player. Also, there can be more than one winner if the players have agreed to such a rule before starting the game (see Section 2.12, page 42).

A player must always know what his or her Winning Tiles are, in order to declare a win whenever one presents itself. A player must be careful not to declare a false win, however, or he or she will be subject to a penalty, which can upset the other players.

After each hand, the tiles are turned face down, mixed well, and the walls are built again, ready for the next hand.

2.8 Failing to Claim a Discard to Declare Pung or a Win

If a player fails to claim a discard to declare Pung, he or she is not permitted to claim the same tile subsequently discarded by the next players until after making his or her own discard.

If a player fails to claim a discard to declare a win, he or she is not permitted to claim the same tile or another Winning Tile subsequently discarded by the next players until after he or she has made a discard. In the Cantonese Game, the Shanghai Game, and the 12-Tile Game, however, the player is permitted to declare a win if he or she subsequently draws the Winning Tile, even before making a discard. But in the 16-Tile Game, a self-drawn tile is treated like a discarded tile in this situation.

Example: You have a No. 2 and No. 3 but fail to claim a No. 1 to declare a win, you cannot claim a No. 1 tile or a No. 4 tile subsequently discarded by the next players until after you have made a discard yourself.

In the Taiwanese Game, if a player misses a chance to claim a discard to declare a win, or discards a Winning Tile by mistake, he or she is not permitted to declare a win by claiming the same tile until making a discard, regardless of whether that same tile is a subsequent discard or a self-drawn tile.

2.9 The Dealer and the Duration of a Game

Each hand of the game always has a Dealer. The Dealer will keep the role until another player wins a hand. In such a case, the dealership is passed on to the Dealer's Lower House. When each player has been Dealer at least once and the fourth Dealer loses the hand, a round of the game is completed. The game will continue in the second round with the first-term Dealer announcing the Wind of the new round. The first round of the game is called the East Round, which is followed by the South Round, the West Round, and the North Round. The game is completed when the last Dealer in the North Round loses his or her hand in the fourth round.

A complete game consists of four rounds. Players may continue the game by starting another four rounds. But the seat allocation procedure and the designation of First Dealer are usually determined all over again.

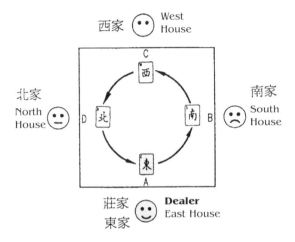

The Dealer of each game is called the East House. Other players will have corresponding titles. The Dealer's Lower House is the South House, the Dealer's Opposite House is the West House, and the Dealer's Upper House is the North House.

During the game, a Round Indicator (Jong), which shows the proper round, is passed to a new Dealer located to his or her right.

The Dealer commences each game by casting the dice to decide which one of the walls is to be broken and which stack of tiles is to be the first stack to be picked up.

Example: The Dealer is seated at side A of the table and casts two dice.

Sum of dots	Wall to be broken
2, 6, 10	B side, the Dealer's Lower House
3, 7, 11	C side, the Dealer's Opposite House
4, 8, 12	D side, the Dealer's Upper House
5, 9	A side, the Dealer him- or herself

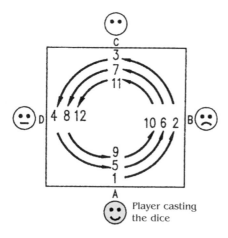

Player casting the dice

If the Dealer is seated at side A of the table and the sum of dots is three, the Dealer picks up stacks No. 4 and No. 5 of wall C. This is followed by the Dealer's Lower House, Opposite House, Upper House, then the Dealer again, and so on. Each takes a turn to pick up two stacks of tiles in the clockwise direction for three turns and one tile in the last turn.

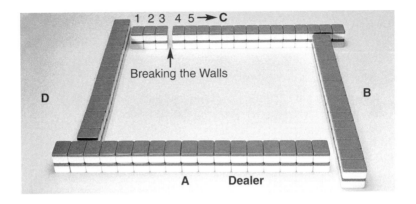

1 2 3 4 5→C

Breaking the Walls

D

B

A   Dealer

2.10 Scoring (Gai Fan) 計番

The score is counted in terms of Fan. A certain number of Fans is given to a certain combination of matched sets in a hand. An easy combination of matched sets has a lower score than a difficult one.

Great variation exists in the combinations of matched sets. The players can choose to limit the type of combinations to be scored, however, and to set the minimum and maximum number of Fans for a winning hand. The following are the most common choices of combinations, with their corresponding scores in the Cantonese Game (Old Rules).

ZERO FAN 無番

0A Gay Woo – Chicken Hand 雞糊

The Chicken Hand consists of both Sequences and Triplets in more than one suit. The "winning" player of this lowest scoring hand does not earn any Fans, but is still rewarded for completing the hand.

ONE FAN 一番

1A Ping Woo – Common Hand 平糊

The Common Hand consists only of Sequences in more than one suit.

1B Fan Jee – Dragon Tiles 番子　中發白

Each Triplet of Dragon tiles earns the winner a Fan. The exception is the presence of more than two Triplets of Dragon tiles in a winning hand (see 3C and 6A).

The Red Dragon (Chung)

The Green Dragon (Fat)

The White Dragon (Bak)

1C Huen Fung – Wind of the Round 圈風

A Triplet of Wind tiles that matches the round of the game is worth a Fan. Huen Fung means a Triplet of East Wind tiles in the East Round (the first round), a Triplet of South Wind tiles in the South Round (the second round), a Triplet of West Wind tiles in the West Round (the third round), or a Triplet of North Wind tiles in the North Round (the fourth round).

1D Moon Fung – House Wind Tiles 門風

A Triplet of Wind tiles that matches the player's position in a round earns the winner a Fan. Moon Fung means a Triplet of East Wind tiles for the Dealer, a Triplet of South Wind tiles for the Dealer's Lower House, a Triplet of West Wind tiles for the Dealer's Opposite House, or a Triplet of North Wind tiles for the Dealer's Upper House.

1E Chi Mo – Self-drawn 自摸

When the winner draws the winning tile from the wall, he earns an extra Fan by Chi Mo.

1F Cheung Gong – Robbing a Gong 搶槓

When the winner claims the winning tile (the fourth identical tile) from another player who has just declared a revealed Gong, he earns an extra Fan by Cheung Gong.

1G Moon Ching – All Concealed Hand 門清

(Note: Moon Ching is not included in the original Old Rules Game. This scoring hand is optional.)

When the winning hand is without any revealed set, the player earns an extra Fan for "keeping his door clean."

1H Dok Ting – Single Way to Win 獨聽

(Note: Dok Ting is not included in the original Old Rules Game. This scoring hand is optional.)

When the player has only one chance to match the winning set or the Eyes, he or she can earn an extra Fan. For example, when the last set to match in making a winning hand consists of a No. 1 tile and a No. 2 tile, then the only way to win is to obtain a No. 3 tile.

The player cannot win the game in any other way. Similarly, if the last set to match contains a No. 4 tile and a No. 6 tile, the only way to win is to obtain a No. 5 tile. Waiting for a tile to complete the Eyes is known as the Dok Ting situation.

winning tiles

1I Far Yiu – Terminal Triplets with Honor Tiles 花么

When a winning hand is a mixture of Terminal Triplets of the Common tiles and one or more Triplets of the Honor tiles, and the Eyes are also a pair of Honor tiles or Terminal tiles, the hand is called Far Yiu. The winner then earns an extra Fan.

TWO FANS 兩番

2A Gong Sheung Far – Added Glory to a Gong 槓上花

The Winning Tile is the make-up tile following a revealed or concealed Gong.

2B Hoi Day – The Last Tile 海底

The Winning Tile is the last drawable tile or the last discard.

(Note: The last 14 tiles on the tail end of the walls are not drawable.)

2C Huen Moon Fung – Prevailing Wind Tiles 圈門風

A winning hand containing a Triplet of Wind tiles when the Wind matches both the player's seating position (see 1D Moon Fung) and the Wind of the round (see 1C Huen Fung). For example, the Dealer has a winning hand containing a Triplet of East Wind tiles in the East Wind Round.

THREE FANS 三番

3A Dui Dui Woo – All Triplets 對對糊

A winning hand consisting of only Triplets and Eyes.

3B Won Yat Sik – Mixed One Suit 混一色

A winning hand consisting of sets from one suit of the Common tiles mixed with Honor tiles.

3C Siu Sam Yuen – Junior 3 Chiefs 小三元

A winning hand consisting of two Triplets plus one pair of Dragon tiles.

3D Gong Sheung Gong – Double Gong 槓上槓

When a player draws or claims a fourth tile to declare a Gong and form a Quadruplet, he or she must draw a make-up tile from the end of the wall. If the make-up tile is the fourth tile of another Triplet, the player declares Gong again and draws another make-up tile from the end of the wall. If the second make-up tile happens to be the Winning Tile of the hand, the situation is called Double Gong. Any winning hand with a Double Gong earns the winner an additional 3 Fans.

3E Hoi Day Lao Yuet – Catching the Moon from the Bottom of the Sea 海底撈月

The self-drawn Winning Tile is the last drawable tile of the wall, which is a No. 1 Circle tile that forms the Eyes with another No. 1 Circle tile in the winning hand. Remember, there are 14 untouchable tiles on the tail ends of the walls.

3F Gong Sheung Mui Far – Plum Blossom on a Gong 槓上梅花

The Winning Tile is a No. 5 Circle tile, which is the make-up tile self-drawn after a Gong. It forms a Sequence with a No. 4 Circle tile and a No. 6 Circle tile.

SIX FANS 六番

6A Dai Sam Yuen – Grand 3 Chiefs 大三元

A winning hand containing three Triplets of Dragon tiles.

6B Siu Sei Hei – Junior 4 Happiness 小四喜

A winning hand containing three Triplets and a pair of Eyes, all composed of Wind tiles.

6C Ching Yat Sik – Pure One Suit 清一色

A winning hand consisting solely of Common tiles in any one suit.

6D Eight Flower Tiles 八隻花

If during the game, a player draws all eight flower tiles, he or she will have a winning hand.

EIGHT FANS 八番

8A Dai Sei Hei – Grand 4 Happiness 大四喜

A winning hand containing all four Triplets of the Wind tiles.

8B Chuen Tse – All Honor Tiles 全字

A winning hand containing four Triplets and the Eyes, all composed of Honor tiles.

8C Kan Kan Woo – All Concealed Triplets 刻刻糊

A winning hand containing four concealed Triplets and the winning tile is self-drawn. (Note: A Quadruplet is not counted as a concealed Triplet in this case.)

8D Sup Sam Yiu – 13 Terminal Tiles 十三么

A winning hand containing one of no. 1 and no. 9 tiles of all three Common suits and one of all the Honor tiles, plus any one matching tile for the Eyes.

8E Tin Woo – Heavenly Hand 天糊

When the Dealer draws the first tile from the wall and this first tile is a winning tile, he or she has a Heavenly Hand.

8F Dei Woo – Earthly Hand 地糊

When the winning tile is claimed from the first discarded tile by the Dealer, the winner has an Earthly Hand.

2.11 Computing the Fans

Fans are summed by all possible scoring combinations in a winning hand.

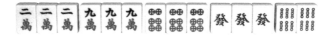

Example 1: An All Triplet Hand containing a Dragon Triplet earns 4 Fans.

3A	All Triplets	:	3 Fans
1B	One Dragon Triplet	:	1 Fan
	Total	:	4 Fans

Example 2: A Mixed One-Suit Hand with two Dragon Triplets earns 5 Fans.

3B	Mixed One Suit	:	3 Fans
2x1B	Two Dragon Triplets	:	2 Fans
	Total	:	5 Fans

Example 3: A winning hand with all Triplets, mixing one suit and two Dragon Triplets, earns 8 Fans.

3A	All Triplets	:	3 Fans
3B	Mixed One Suit	:	3 Fans
2x1B	Two Dragon Triplets	:	2 Fans
	Total	:	8 Fans

Example 4: A winning hand with all Triplets, mixing one suit and Junior 3 Chiefs, earns 9 Fans.

3A	All Triplets	:	3 Fans
3B	Mixed One Suit	:	3 Fans
3C	Junior 3 Chiefs	:	3 Fans
	Total	:	9 Fans

Example 5: A winning hand with four Sequences and the Eyes all in one suit earns 7 Fans.

6C	Pure One Suit	:	6 Fans
1A	All Sequences	:	1 Fan
	Total	:	7 Fans

Example 6: A winning hand with all Triplets and the Eyes in one suit earns 9 Fans.

6C	Pure One Suit	:	6 Fans
3A	All Triplets	:	3 Fans
	Total	:	9 Fans

Example 7: A mixed One Suit, All Triplet Hand with Grand 3 Chiefs (all three Dragon Triplets) and a self-drawn Winning Tile earns 13 Fans.

3B	Mixed One Suit	:	3 Fans
3A	All Triplets	:	3 Fans
6A	Grand 3 Chiefs	:	6 Fans
1E	Self-drawn	:	1 Fan
	Total	:	13 Fans

2.12 Awarding the Winner

When playing the Cantonese Game, the rule of choosing awards must be agreed upon by all the players prior to the game. There will be only one winner in each hand of the game. If there is more than one player claiming the same discarded tile to complete the winning hand, then the Lower House of the discarder has higher priority than the other players. The Upper House has the lowest priority.

2.12.1 Jit Woo – To Intercept a Winning Hand 截糊

Stealing the winning chance from the players with lower priority by interception is called Jit Woo. This happens quite often when two players claim the same discarded tile to complete winning hands. Sometimes the player with lower priority has a much higher-scoring hand than that of the interceptor. This unfortunate paradox can be upsetting for the higher-scoring player.

In the Cantonese Game, the method of determining the winner's awards is intended to motivate the players to reach the highest possible score. The formula for awards enables the winner to double his or her award for each additional Fan when the total score is four Fans or less, and for every two additional Fans for five Fans or higher. The award is given in points. A point can be of any value agreed upon by the players prior to the game.

2.12.2 Table of Awards

No. of Fans of the winner	Full Score (points)	One-Half of Full Score (points)
0	2	1
1	4	2
2	8	4
3	16	8
4	32	16
5	48	24
6	64	32
7	96	48
8	128	64
9	192	96
10	256	128
11	384	192
12	512	256

4-Fans is called Moon Woo (Full Woo)   滿糊

6-Fans is called Seung Lart (Double Hot)   雙辣

8-Fans is called Sam Lart (Triple Hot)   三辣

10-Fans is called Sei Lart (Quadruple Hot)   四辣

12-Fans is called Ung Lart (Quintuple Hot)   五辣

2.13 Paying the Winner

Of course, as with any game, the winner should be rewarded. But who should pay the winner or winners? And how much? The players can choose *one* of the following ways to pay the winner:

(1) Only the discarder pays the winner one full score.

(2) Only the discarder pays the winner two times the full score.

(3) The discarder pays the winner the full score, and each of the other two players pays the winner one-half of the full score.

(4) In the event of (1) or (2), when a player claims the fourth identical tile discarded by another player to declare a Concealed Gong, and the make-up tile is the Winning Tile of his or her winning hand, then the discarder of the fourth identical tile pays the winner three times the full score.

If the Winning Tile is self-drawn, the other three players each pay the winner one full score.

2.14 Bao – Penalty to the Risk Taker 包

Under each of the following situations, the discarder of the Winning Tile must pay the winner a total of two times the full score, for him- or herself and the other two players:

Bao Fan Jee 包番子

(a) Grand 3 Chiefs Hand: One player has revealed two sets of Dragon Triplets and another player (the risk taker) discards the third Dragon tile, which turns out to be the Winning Tile of a Grand 3 Chiefs Hand.

(b) Grand 4 Happiness Hand: One player has revealed three sets of Wind Triplets and the risk taker discards the fourth Wind tile, which turns out to be the Winning Tile of a Grand 4 Happiness Hand.

(c) All Honor Tiles Hand: One player has revealed three sets of Honor tiles (in combination with Wind and Dragon tiles), and the risk taker discards any Honor tile, which turns out to be the Winning Tile of an All Honor Tiles Hand.

Bao Yiu Kau 包么九

(d) All Terminal Triplets Hand: One player has revealed three sets of Terminal Triplets, and the risk taker discards any Terminal tile, which turns out to be the Winning Tile of an All Terminal Triplets Hand.

Bao Kau Jeung 包九張

(e) Pure One-Suit Hand: One player has revealed three sets of tiles of the same suit and the risk taker discards a tile of the same suit, which turns out to be the Winning Tile of a Pure One-Suit Hand.

The following situations are also involved with risk taking, but the penalty is different:

Bao Sup Yee Jeung 包十二張

(f) Same as the situations in (c), (d), or (e), but the discarded tile is not the Winning Tile. Instead, the discarded tile made by the risk taker is a matching tile of the fourth set in the same suit. The situation then becomes more complicated:

A. If the player with four revealed sets draws the Winning Tile, then the risk taker must pay the winner for all the other players as well as for him- or herself. This will amount to three times the full score.

B. If the player with four revealed sets subsequently claims the Winning Tile from another discarded by the risk taker, the risk taker must pay the winner for all the other players as well as for him- or herself. This will amount to only two times the full score.

C. If the player with four revealed sets subsequently claims the Winning Tile from a discard by a third player (that is, not the risk taker), then both the risk taker and the third player must pay the winner one full score each.

Bao Sang Jeung 包生張

(g) When there are only five drawable tiles remaining on the table, and a player discards a Winning Tile that has not been discarded or revealed earlier, the discarder must pay the winner for all the other players as well as for him or her self.

Bao Sin Ung Bao Hau 包先唔包後

(h) If two players have each revealed three sets of tiles in one suit (for example, Player A reveals three sets of Circle tiles and, later, Player B reveals three sets of Bamboo tiles), and it happens that Player C has only Circle and Bamboo tiles remaining in his or her playing hand, Player C will not be penalized in payment for all the other players even if he discards the winning tile to Player B. This holds true if Player C has not claimed any discards after Players A and B have each revealed three sets of tiles of the same suit. But Player C will be penalized if he or she discards the Winning Tile to Player A.

2.15 Penalties 罰

2.15.1 Falsely Declaring a Win (Jar Woo) 詐糊

If a player declares a win by claiming a discarded tile or by drawing a tile, and it turns out that his hand is not yet ready for the win, then the win has been falsely declared. In this case, he or she must pay each of the other three players an amount equivalent to four Fans.

2.15.2 Long or Short Hand
(Dai Sheong Kung, Siu Sheong Kung) 大相公, 小相公

If, during a game, a player finds that his or her playing hand is either more, or less, than 13 tiles, the player is not allowed to discard the excessive tile or to draw a make-up tile to complete the hand. Instead, he or she must continue to play by drawing and discarding tiles as usual until the game is over. This player must be careful in discarding tiles. To avoid losing to a high-scoring hand, he or she should discard only nonmatching tiles to other players, in the hope that no opponent will win the game by claiming one of the discards.

2.16 Fortune Hand – a Draw (Wong Pai) 旺牌

When only seven stacks (14 tiles) are left on the wall, with none of the players being able to complete a winning hand, the game is considered a draw. This is called a Fortune Hand because there is no loser. The same Dealer will continue for the next game.

2.17 Playing with Flower Tiles (Dar Far) 打花

In addition to the 136 basic tiles, a set of mahjong also contains 8 Flower Tiles, comprising two sets of 4 tiles. The 4 tiles in one set represent the four seasons, while the 4 tiles in the other set represent the blossoms or plants of the 4 seasons.

Set One   Set Two

No. 1: Spring   No. 1: Plum
No. 2: Summer   No. 2: Orchid
No. 3: Autumn   No. 3: Chrysanthemum
No. 4: Winter   No. 4: Bamboo

Playing with the Flower tiles is optional. Flower tiles score additional Fans for the winning hand.

When building the walls, the Flower tiles are mixed with the other tiles. Each player will then stack up a row of 18 pairs of tiles instead of 17 pairs. A playing hand still contains 13 tiles, however. After the initial 13 tiles are drawn from the walls, each player reveals all the Flower tiles contained in the initial selection by placing them face up on the table. Then the exchange process begins. Starting with the Dealer, each player in turn draws a make-up tile from the end of the wall for each revealed Flower tile. If the make-up tile happens to be another Flower tile, the player immediately draws another make-up tile from the end of the wall. (In the 16-Tile Game, the player must wait until all the other players have drawn their make-up tiles in their normal turns.) Similarly, during the course of the game, when a player draws a Flower tile from the wall, he or she reveals it and immediately draws a make-up tile from the end of the wall. At no time is a Flower tile allowed to be kept in a playing hand. Moreover, if the player forgets to draw a make-up tile to replace the revealed Flower tile, he or she is not permitted to draw a make-up tile after a discard has been made. In that case, the hand will be a tile short, known as a Short Hand (see Section 2.15.2). The player is therefore unable to complete his or her hand to win the game.

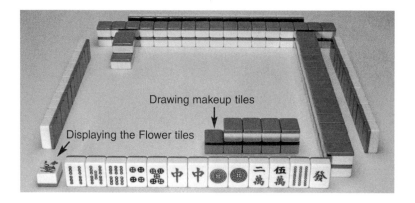

Drawing makeup tiles

Displaying the Flower tiles

2.17.1 Scoring for Flower Tiles

Each Flower tile adds a Fan to the winning hand. Nevertheless, the players should agree upon the method of counting Fans and scoring prior to starting the game. The following are the common methods of scoring Flower tiles:

A. The possession of each Flower tile, or the absence of Flower tiles, is counted as one Fan.

B. The possession of any of the Flower tiles that matches the round of game is counted as one Fan.

Flower tiles that match the round of the game:

No. 1: Flower tiles during the first round (East Round).

No. 2: Flower tiles during the second round (South Round).

No. 3: Flower tiles during the third round (West Round).

No. 4: Flower tiles during the fourth round (North Round).

C. The possession of any of the Flower tiles that matches the respective position of the player is counted as one Fan.

Flower tiles that match the respective position of the players:

No. 1: Flower tiles in the hand of the Dealer.

No. 2: Flower tiles in the hand of the Dealer's Lower House.

No. 3: Flower tiles in the hand of the Dealer's Opposite House.

No. 4: Flower tiles in the hand of the Dealer's Upper House.

D. The possession of any of the Flower tiles that matches both the round of the game and the respective position of the players is counted as two Fans.

No. 1: Flower tiles in the hand of the Dealer during the first round, No. 2: Flower tiles in the hand of the Dealer's Lower House (the South House) during the second round of the game, and so on.

Any player who accumulates all eight Flower tiles during the game, is considered to have completed his or her hand and thus wins the game.

Note: When a player has accumulated seven Flower tiles, he or she can claim the eighth Flower tile previously or subsequently drawn from the walls from any player to win the game. The drawer of the eighth Flower tile is considered the discarder of the Winning Tile.

2.18 Five-Player Game – Dreaming (Dar Mung) 打懵

Mahjong is normally a four-player game, but five players can play it by rotation.

During the allotment of seats at the beginning of the game, a No. 5 Circle tile is added to the four Wind tiles to make a five-tile stack. The four players who pick the Wind tiles will start the game. The person who picks the No. 5 Circle tile must wait an entire round before he or she can participate. Since the fifth player has little to do, he or she is aptly called a Dreamer.

At the end of the first round (East Wind Round), the First Dealer retires and is replaced by the fifth player, the Dreamer. The retired First Dealer becomes a Dreamer for the second round. At the end of this round (South Wind Round), the South player is replaced by the First Dealer. The game continues until five rounds have been reached, with each player having participated in four of the five. If desired, the game can continue uninterrupted by repeating the same procedure. The seat reallotment is not required after each five-round cycle.

2.19 Three-Player Game (Dar Sam Yan Pai) 打三人牌

The game can be played as well in the absence of one player, by removing any one suit of the tiles from the set. However, when casting the dice to designate the First Dealer and to break the walls in each game, if the count ends at the absentee player, the dice must be cast again.

CHAPTER THREE

BASIC STRATEGY

Mahjong is usually regarded as an offensive, rather than a defensive, game. Nonetheless, a player is required to know how to discard tiles safely and wisely. In order to do this, every player must try to recognize the types of hands his or her opponents are likely to be matching by observing closely what tiles they discard.

3.1 Speed

A player should try to complete his hand ahead of the other players in the shortest possible time. This is done by choosing, from the tiles in the existing hand, combinations that are most likely to be completed in a short time. Do not attempt to assemble a high-scoring hand when the chance of completing it is remote.

3.2 Taking Advantage of Opportunities

◆ Saving and matching the same suit of tiles that your Upper House is frequently discarding.

◆ When your hand has six or more tiles of the same suit, plus Honor tiles, consider assembling a Mixed One-Suit Hand.

◆ When your hand consists of two or more pairs, consider assembling an All Triplets Hand.

◆ When your hand has nine or more Terminal and Honor tiles, consider assembling a 13-Terminal Tile hand.

◆ Be prepared to change the combination in your hand according to the types of tiles drawn from the walls or discarded by others.

3.3 Keeping Alert

◆ If possible, do not discard tiles of the same suit that your Lower House is saving and claiming.

◆ When a player has revealed two or more sets of the same suit (with or without Honor tiles), he or she is probably trying to assemble a Pure One-Suit or a Mixed One-Suit Hand.

◆ When a player has revealed two or more Triplets, he or she is probably trying to assemble an All Triplets Hand.

◆ When a player discards Honor tiles late in the game, he or she is probably matching a high-scoring hand.

◆ When a player discards tiles of two suits only, he or she is saving the other suit of the Common tiles.

◆ When a player discards Terminal tiles and Honor tiles at an early stage of the game, he or she is most likely trying to complete a low-scoring hand quickly. Do not waste your time assembling a high-scoring hand.

3.4 Safe Discards

◆ When you decide to assemble a Mixed One-Suit or Pure One-Suit Hand, discard the sharp tiles (tiles that are easy to match such as Nos. 2 to 8) of your unwanted suits as early as possible, before your Lower House saves enough matched tiles to claim your discards.

◆   When you sense a dangerous situation, such as one player assembling a high-scoring hand, you should immediately try to help other players win a lower-scoring hand by discarding the tiles the other players might need.

◆   Prolonging the game in order to assemble a high-scoring hand when the situation is tense is unwise. Be satisfied with a lower-scoring hand. After all, winning, rather than score counting, is the ultimate objective.

◆   When the game is near its end without a winner yet, consider giving up your chance of winning by discarding only the safe tiles.

◆   When appropriate, use Pung or Gong to disrupt other players from claiming a matched tile or drawing a tile.

3.5 Improving Your Winning Chance

◆   When you are waiting for the final matched tile to complete your winning hand, call for the tiles that other players feel safe to discard.

◆   Exchange your tiles to increase the probability of winning. For example, if your hand calls for a No. 4 tile to win, such as the following hand:

If you draw a No. 6 tile, you should discard the No. 3 tile and keep your drawn tile. Now you have three winning chances instead of one. Your Winning Tile can be No. 4, No. 5, or No. 7.

With a No. 4 tile, your winning match would be

With a No. 5 tile, your winning match would be

With a No. 7 tile, your winning match would be

3.6 Improving Your Hand for a Higher Score

Example 1: From a Chicken Hand to an All Sequences Hand

If you draw a No. 4 or No. 6 Bamboo tile, discard the No. 5 tile, and you have

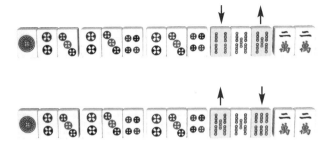

Now you are calling either No. 3 or No. 6, or either No. 4 or No. 7.

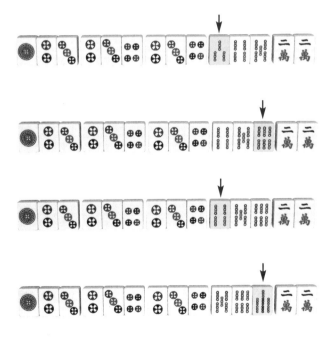

Example 2: From a Chicken Hand to an All Triplets Hand

If you draw or claim a No. 4 Circle tile, discard the No. 1 tile,

rearrange your tiles and you have three Triplets and two pairs.

3.7 Winning Probabilities

Ready Hand

Winning Tiles
(can be any one of the tiles)

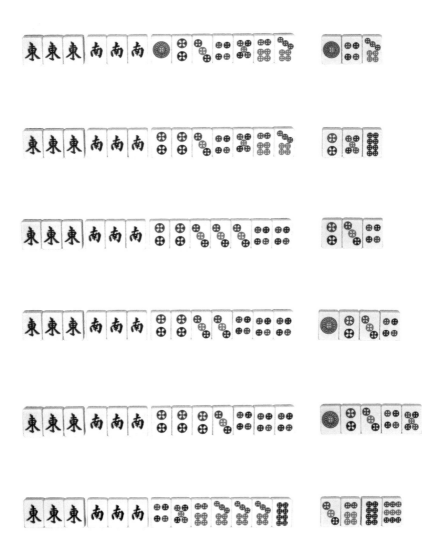

Ready Hand   Winning Tiles
                                     (can be any one of the tiles)

CHAPTER FOUR

COURTESIES

Playing mahjong is meant to be fun. Like all games, some basic disciplines should be observed to make the game more enjoyable. Before starting the players should agree on the rules of the game, including the following:

- The minimum and maximum number of Fans of a winning hand.
- The method of scoring.
- The number of rounds to be played.
- The number of winners allowable in any single game.
- Whether or not the nondiscarder pays the winner.
- Whether or not the Dealer remains the Dealer after a Fortune hand.
- The number of tiles to be left untouched on the wall when a game seems to come to a draw.
- The number of dice to be used.
- The penalty for falsely declaring a win.

Other common rules and courtesies of mahjong include the following:

◆ Be on time.

◆ Always keep calm. Never get too excited or upset.

◆ Do not withdraw from the game before the number of rounds is completed.

◆ Turn all the tiles face down and mix them well before building the walls.

◆ Count the stacks of tiles while building the walls.

◆ Immediately after the drawing of the initial 13 tiles is completed, count the tiles in your hand.

◆ Cast the dice inside the walls and only after the walls are built.

◆ Use only the right hand to draw a tile from the wall or to retrieve a discarded tile.

◆ Keep up speed in drawing and discarding tiles.

◆ Sort and rearrange your hand of tiles only when you are waiting for your turn. Constantly review your hand and consider your next discard tiles, to avoid making other players wait.

◆ Display your revealed sets face up on the table to your left.

◆ Always declare a warning when you have 3 revealed sets of the same suit.

◆ Frequently push the wall of tiles toward the center of the table, so that other players can reach them easily.

- Do not draw before your Upper House discards.

- Gently place discards face up on the table inside the walls.

- When your luck is down, never slam your discards down on the table in a display of temper.

- Do not complain about having a poor playing hand.

- Do not complain when other players discard tiles that are not useful to you.

- Do not change your mind when claiming a discard.

- Do not change your mind by reclaiming your discard.

- Do not declare Pung, Gong or Sik after another player has drawn a tile from the wall following the last discard.

- Do not change your mind after declaring Pung or Gong.

- If you forget to draw a make-up tile from the end of the wall to replace a Flower tile or after declaring a Gong, you cannnot draw a make-up tile after your Lower House has drawn a tile from the wall or claimed a discard.

- If you fail to declare Pung, you are not allowed to claim the same tile subsequently discarded by other players. You can declare pung only after you have made a discard.

- The winner of each hand of the game must be rewarded by the losers immediately, as any unpaid debt is believed to bring bad luck to the winner.

◆ Never leave the table during each set of four rounds of the game (especially during the West Round). Interrupting the game is also believed to bring bad luck to the winner but good luck to the interrupter.

◆ Do not discuss your own or another player's hand or hint at someone's strategy during the game.

◆ Onlookers shall not give advice to the players nor discuss the game.

◆ After each round of the game, the North House should change the Jong Indicator to display the new round of the game.

CHAPTER FIVE

THE SHANGHAI GAME
新章 上海牌

The Shanghai Game, also known as the New Rules Game, is a variation from the Old Rules, or Cantonese Game. The playing of the game is basically the same as the Cantonese Game, but some of the rituals and procedures, such as designating the seating, choosing the First Dealer, building the walls, discarding the tiles, displaying a revealed Sequence, the Fortune Hand, and the matching of the revealed 13-Terminal Tile Hand, are slightly different. The scoring of the Shanghai Game differs substantially from that of the Cantonese Game, in that the former has a much greater variation in the combination of tiles and sets in a winning hand. Certain terminologies are different, too, and the terms are pronounced in Mandarin Chinese, instead of in Cantonese.

Due to the complexity of its scoring, the Shanghai Game is not recommended for beginners. In this chapter, the author assumes that the reader is already familiar with certain basic procedures, such as claiming a tile to match a Sequence or a Triplet, and the general courtesies that must be observed during the game.

5.1 Terminology

There are some slight differences in terminology between the Shanghai Game and the Cantonese Game:

	Cantonese	Shanghai
(1) Claiming a tile to match a Sequence:	Sheung 上	Chuh 食
(2) Claiming a tile to match a Triplet:	Pung 碰	Peng 碰
(3) Claiming a tile for a Quadruplet:	Gong 槓	Garng 槓
(4) Claiming a tile to win:	Sik 食	Hu 胡

5.2 Designating the Chair of the First Dealer 搬位

Once the four players have seated themselves randomly around a square table, any player may cast two or three dice, and the dots are summed. The dice caster begins to count counterclockwise with his or her seat counted as 1, the next seat as 2, and so forth, until the sum is reached. The seat at the end of the count is the chair of the First Dealer.

Example: If the player at Side A of the table casts the dice and the sum of the dots is two, then Side B is the chair of the First Dealer and is also the East chair of the first round.

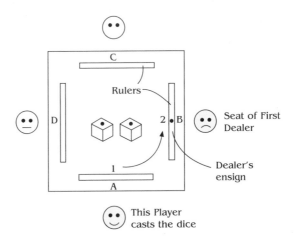

5.3 Choosing the First Dealer 打莊

Just as in the Cantonese Game, one each of the four Wind tiles is used for choosing the First Dealer. Unlike the Cantonese Game, the four Wind tiles are mixed well and placed face down in a row on the table. Furthermore, a No. 1 tile is placed face up on the left end of the row, and a No. 2 tile is placed, face up on the right end.

Then the same player casts the dice again to determine who will pick up the first Wind tile in the row. If the sum of the dots on the cast dice is an odd number, the player at the end of the count picks up the first Wind tile from the end having the No. 1 tile. If the sum is an even number, then the first Wind tile is picked up from the opposite end. The Lower House of the first Wind tile picker then picks up the second Wind tile and so forth.

Example: If the sum of the dots on the cast dice is three (an odd number), the player at side C picks up the first Wind tile from the end that has the No. 1 tile.

If the sum of the dots on the cast dice is two (an even number), the player at side B picks up the first Wind tile from the end that has the No. 2 tile.

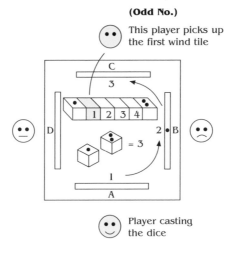

(Odd No.)

This player picks up the first wind tile

Player casting the dice

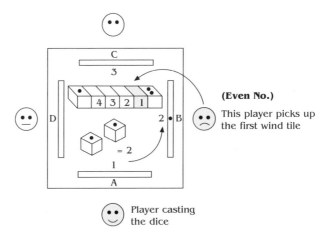

(Even No.)

This player picks up the first wind tile

Player casting the dice

After four Wind tiles have been picked up, the player who holds the East Wind tile is designated as the First Dealer, and he or she is seated at the East Chair, as designated by the previous cast of the dice. The player who holds the South Wind tile is seated to the right of the East chair. The players who hold the West Wind tile and the North Wind tile will be seated, respectively opposite the East side and to the left of the East side.

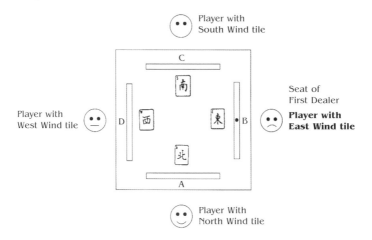

In the Shanghai Game, after the first four rounds of the game have been completed, the players do not have to undergo the same long procedure of choosing and designating the seating all over again. Instead, they merely exchange seats: East with South and North with West. The last winner of the fourth round will be the First Dealer of the next four rounds. But after eight rounds are completed, the process of seat selection is carried out as a new round.

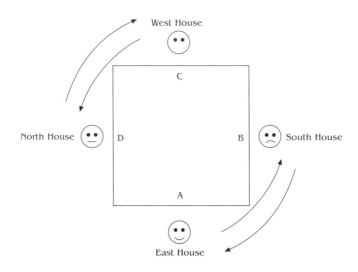

5.4 Building the Walls (De Pai) 疊牌

For the Shanghai Game, the walls of tiles are arranged in two single rows of 17 tiles each. These rows are placed in contact with each other, instead of being stacked up, in the style of the Cantonese Game. In the Shanghai Game, the row that is located near the table center is equivalent to the upper row of the double stack in the Cantonese Game. Usually, a set of four rulers, each having a length equal to 18 tiles, is provided for each player to align the tiles when building the walls. One of the rulers is engraved with the First Dealer's ensign. This ruler should be used by the First Dealer for identification. The rulers are also used by the players during the game to keep the playing-hand tiles tidy.

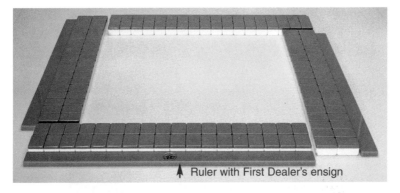

Ruler with First Dealer's ensign

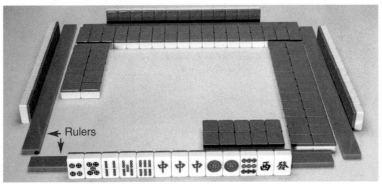

Rulers

5.5 Discards (Chu Pai) 出牌

Discarded tiles should be arranged in rows in an orderly fashion inside the walls in front of each player.

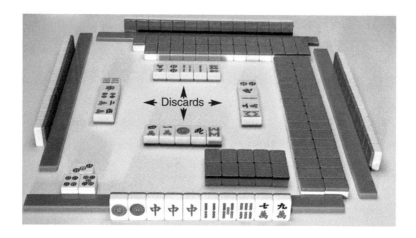

5.6 Displaying Revealed Sequences

When a player claims a discard to make a Sequence, he or she reveals the 2 matched tiles face up and side by side on the table. The player then places the claimed tile in contact with both of the 2 revealed matched tiles, away from him- or herself, in a horizontal position. By doing so, the claimed discard can be identified.

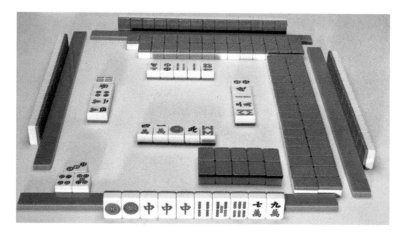

5.7 Fortune Hand (Wang Zhuang) 旺莊

All of the tiles on the walls are available for drawing to complete the game. If there is no winner as the last tile is drawn and a discard is made, a Fortune Hand has been played, since there is no loser in the hand. With the Shanghai Game, the dealership is passed on to the next player. This is different from the Cantonese Game, in which the dealership is passed on to the next player only when there is a winner.

5.8 Assembling a Revealed 13-Terminal Tile Hand (Wai Shuh San Yiao) 外十三么

In the Shanghai Game, a player is also allowed to assemble on the table a 13-Terminal Tile Hand with his discards while still reserving the right of matching a concealed hand.

Unlike the 13-Terminal Tile Hand that is assembled, unrevealed, in a playing hand, this "revealed" 13-Terminal Tile Hand is made by continuously discarding one each of the 13-Terminal tiles and Honor tiles without interruption. These discarded tiles are displayed in a row inside the wall in front of the player. Note: The discarding of Terminal tiles cannot be interrupted by discarding a non-Terminal tile or by claiming a discard from another player. If another player claims any of the discarded Terminal or Honor tiles (other than to declare a win) in this "revealed" 13-Terminal Tile Hand in the making, those claimed discards will still be counted as part of the 13 Terminal tiles needed for completing the hand. Of course, the player must keep track of which Terminal tiles were claimed by whom, so that those claimed tiles can be reclaimed to complete a winning hand.

The winner of the 13-Terminal Tile Hand has first priority to claim a Winning Tile regardless of which player discards it.

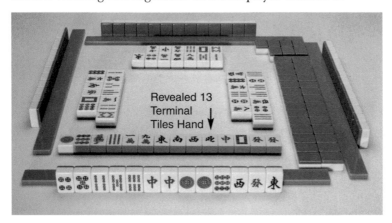

Revealed 13 Terminal Tiles Hand

5.9 Scoring (Suan Fan) 算番

Scoring in the Shanghai Game is quite different from the Cantonese Game. For instance, the lowest score (the minimum hand) and the highest score (the limited hand) are usually set by the players before starting each game. In general, the minimum hand is set at 5 Fans, while the limiting hand is 100 Fans (Fung Men) or 200 Fans (Shuang Fung Men). Beginners may find it more desirable to lower the minimum hand to 3 Fans for an easier win and to make learning the game more interesting.

ONE FAN 一番

1A Jiang – Special Eyes 將

Eyes composed of No. 2, No. 5, or No. 8 tiles of any suit.

TWO FANS 兩番

2A Ping Hu – All Sequences Hand 平糊

A winning hand consisting only of Sequences in more than one suit.

2B Chueh Yi Men – Absence of One Suit 缺一門

A winning hand consisting of Sequences and Triplets in two suits, with or without the Honor tiles.

2C Duan Yiao – Absence of Terminal Tiles 斷么

A winning hand that does not contain any No. 1, or No. 9 tiles or an Honor tile.

2D Yi Ban Gao – Two Identical Sequences 一般高

A winning hand consisting of two identical Sequences.

2E Men Chien Ching – Without Revealed Sets 門前清

A winning hand completed without claiming any discard (claiming a discard for a Quadruplet is not considered claiming a discard in this case).

2F Duh Ting – One Way to Win 獨聽

Only one number can be the Winning Tile.

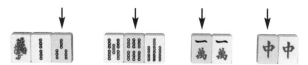

2G Garng – Following a Garng 槓上花

The Winning Tile is the make-up tile following a Garng.

2H Fung – Honor Tiles 三元牌 圈風 門風

A Triplet of Dragon, Round Wind, or House Wind tiles.

2I Ching Szu Peng – Four Revealed Triplets 清四碰

A winning hand with four revealed Triplets.

2J Lao Shao – Young and Old Sequences 老少

A winning hand containing one Sequence of No. 1, No. 2, and No. 3, and another Sequence of No. 7, No. 8, and No. 9, both of the same suit.

2K Kan Shin Wu – Bridge Tile 嵌心五

When the Winning Tile is the No. 5 tile, which completes a Sequence, together with the No. 4 and No. 6 tiles, in any suit (Kan Shin Wu and Duh Ting (2F) is four Fans).

THREE FANS 三番

3A Lao Shao Peng – Young and Old Triplets 老少碰

A winning hand containing one Triplet of No. 1 and another Triplet of No. 9 tiles of the same suit.

3B Liang Garng – Two Quadruplets 兩槓

A winning hand containing two Quadruplets of any suit.

3C Chiang Garng – Robbing a Garng 搶槓

Claiming the Winning Tile from another player who declares a Garng, at the time he or she adds the fourth identical tile to a revealed Triplet.

3D Hai Dee – Last Tile Drawn 海底

A self-drawn Winning Tile that is the last one on the walls.

3E Hai Di Chong – Last Tile Drawn and Discarded 海底銃

The Winning Tile is the last tile drawn from the walls and immediately discarded by another player.

3F Jueh Jarng – One Tile to Win 絕張

When only one number can win and the Winning Tile is the final tile of that number, as three out of four of the same number have already been discarded and therefore revealed.

3G Szu Gui Er – Four into Two 四歸二

Four tiles of the same number tiles included in two sets, a Sequence and a Triplet.

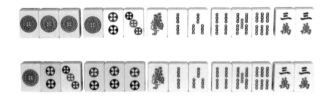

3H Wei Wei – A Tail 尾尾

Two triplets plus one pair in consecutive numbers of the same suit, or two sets and one pair of any Wind tiles.

FIVE FANS 五番

5A Men Ching Buh Chiu – Totally Self-Sufficient 門清不求

An All Concealed Hand, achieved without claiming any discard and the Winning Tile is self-drawn. Note: Quadruplets are counted as a concealed set.

SEVEN FANS 七番

7A Yi Tiao Long – One Dragon Suit 一條龍

A complete set of numbers, from one to nine, of any one suit.

7B San Xiang Fung – Encounter of Three
(also called Jieh May Hua) 三相逢 （姐妹花）

Three Sequences of the same numbers but in all three suits.

7C Huen Dai Yiao – Mixed Terminal Sequences and
Honor Tiles 混帶么

A winning hand with Honor tiles and Sequences (each of which contains a Terminal tile). The Eyes are either composed of Terminal tiles or Honor tiles.

7D Barn Chiu Ren – Semi Self-Sufficient 半求人

A winning hand with four revealed sets and the Winning Tile is self-drawn.

7E Bao Ting – Announcing a Ready Hand 報聽

At the initial drawing of the 13 tiles, and before drawing and claiming any tile, a player announces that he or she has a Ready Hand and is waiting for the Winning Tile. Note: After the announcement, a player cannot exchange any tile in his or her hand with any drawn tile or discard. Failing to do so will forfeit the status of Bao Ting.

7F Wu Men Chih – All Categories 五門齊

A winning hand consisting of all three suits, Wind, and Dragon tiles.

7G Shuang Jueh Jarng – Double Jeopardy 雙絕張

The Winning Tile is the last one of the eight tiles.

Example: The last set you need to complete is composed of No. 2 and No. 3 Circle tiles, and you are waiting either for a No. 1 or No. 4 to win. But all of the No. 1 Circle tiles and three of the four No. 4 tiles have been discarded or revealed.

7H San An Kan – Three Concealed Triplets 三暗刻

A winning hand with three concealed Triplets. Note: A Quadruplet is counted as a concealed Triplet.

7I Huen Yi Sher – Mixed One Suit 混一色

A Mixed One-Suit Hand, which consists of only one suit and Honor tiles.

7J Jieh May Pung – Three Sisters 姐妹碰

Three Triplets of consecutive numbers of the same suit.

7K Szu Gui San – Four into Three 四歸三

Four identical tiles included in two sequences and one pair.

7L Dui Dui Hu – All Triplets 對對糊

An All Triplets Hand.

TEN FANS 十番

10A Chuan Chiu Ren – Total Dependency 全求人

Tiles in all sets and the Eyes being claimed from discards.

10B Ching Yiao – All Terminal Sets 清么

A winning hand without Honor tiles, with each Sequence including a Terminal tile of No. 1 or No. 9.

FIFTEEN FANS 十五番

15A San Garng – Three Quadruplets 三槓

Three Quadruplets, of any tiles or numbers.

15B Tai Ban Gao – Three Identical Sequences 太般高

Three Sequences of the same suit having the same numbers.

15C San Fung Hui – Encounter of 3 Winds 三風會

Three Triplets of Wind tiles.

15D Liang Tiao Long – Two Dragon Suits 兩條龍

A complete set of numbers from one to nine, plus a Sequence of the numbers four, five, and six of the same suit.

TWENTY FANS 二十番

20A Xiao San Yuan – Junior 3 Chiefs 小三元

Two Triplets plus one pair of Dragon tiles.

20B Shuang Piao – Double Lao-Shao 雙飄

Two sets of two Sequences in different suits, each set having a Sequence of No. 1, No. 2, and No. 3 and a Sequence of No. 7, No. 8, and No. 9.

THIRTY FANS 三十番

30A San Shu – Three Numbers 三數

A hand consisting of only tiles of any three numbers, in a Sequence or as Triplets. Note: Dragon or Wind tiles are also counted as one number.

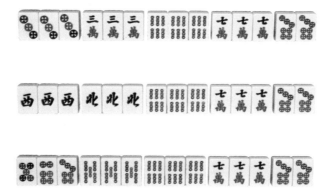

30B Chuan Dai – All Linked 全帶

All linked tiles, every set and the Eyes containing a common number (for example, No. 3).

FORTY FANS 四十番

40A Ching Yi Sher – Pure One Suit 清一色

All tiles of the same suit.

40B Shuang Long Bao Ju – Two Dragons Embracing a Pearl 雙龍抱珠

Two pairs of identical Sequences.

40C Szu Gui Szu – Four into Four 四歸四

Four identical tiles distributed in four Sequences (No. 6 tile).

FIFTY FANS 五十番

50A Szu An Kan – Four Concealed Triplets 四暗刻

Four concealed Triplets. Note: A Quadruplet is counted as a concealed Triplet.

50B Huen Yiao Dui – Mixed Terminal Triplets 混么對

A winning hand consisting of only Honor tiles and Terminal Triplets.

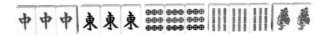

SIXTY FANS 六十番

60A Dah San Yuan – Grand 3 Chiefs 大三元

Three Triplets of Dragon tiles.

60B Xiao Szu Xi – Junior 4 Happiness 小四喜

Three Triplets and a pair of Wind tiles.

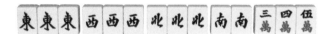

60C Chuan Dai San Shu – All linked with Three Numbers 全帶三數

An All Sequence Hand consisting solely of only of any three numbers.

ONE HUNDRED FANS 一百番
100A Dah Szu Xi – Grand 4 Happiness 大四喜

Four Triplets of Wind tiles.

100B Jiang Jiang Pung 將將碰

An All Triplets Hand including the Eyes, composed of No. 2, No. 5, and No. 8.

100C Ching Yiao Dui – All Terminal Sets 清么對

An All Terminal Triplets Hand.

100D Chuan Dai Yi – All Contain One 全帶一

All Sequences and the Eyes, each containing a No. 1 tile.

100E Chuan Dai Jiu – All Contain Nine 全帶九

All Sequences and the Eyes, each containing a No. 9 tile.

100F Chuan Tsu – All Honor Tiles 全字

100G Tian Hu – Heavenly Hand 天糊

This happens only when the Dealer completes and wins the hand upon drawing his or her first tile from the wall.

100H Dee Hu – Earthly Hand 地糊

The Winning Tile is the first tile discarded by the Dealer.

100I Liang Shu – Two Numbers 兩數

An All Triplets Hand consisting of tiles of only two numbers.
Note: All Wind or Dragon tiles are considered as one number.

100J Shuh Bar Luo Han – 18 Giants 十八羅漢

Four Quadruplets from any tile or suit.

100K Shuh San Yiao – 13 Terminal Tiles 十三么

A winning hand consisting of one each of the No. 1 and No. 9 tiles
of all three suits, plus one each of all the Honor tiles and one
additional matching tile for the Eye.

5.10 Computing the Fans (the Shanghai Game)

Example 1:

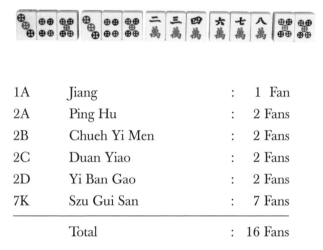

1A	Jiang	:	1 Fan
2A	Ping Hu	:	2 Fans
2B	Chueh Yi Men	:	2 Fans
2C	Duan Yiao	:	2 Fans
2D	Yi Ban Gao	:	2 Fans
7K	Szu Gui San	:	7 Fans
	Total	:	16 Fans

Example 2:

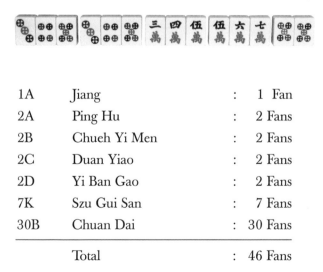

1A	Jiang	:	1 Fan
2A	Ping Hu	:	2 Fans
2B	Chueh Yi Men	:	2 Fans
2C	Duan Yiao	:	2 Fans
2D	Yi Ban Gao	:	2 Fans
7K	Szu Gui San	:	7 Fans
30B	Chuan Dai	:	30 Fans
	Total	:	46 Fans

Example 3:

1A	Jiang	:	1	Fan
2A	Ping Hu	:	2	Fans
2B	Chueh Yi Men	:	2	Fans
2C	Duan Yiao	:	2	Fans
7K	Szu Gui San	:	7	Fans
40B	Shuang Long Bao Ju	:	40	Fans
	Total	:	54	Fans

Example 4:

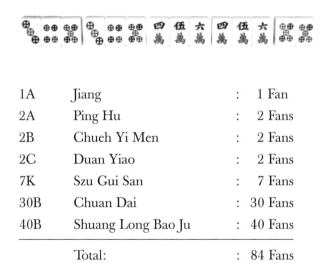

1A	Jiang	:	1	Fan
2A	Ping Hu	:	2	Fans
2B	Chueh Yi Men	:	2	Fans
2C	Duan Yiao	:	2	Fans
7K	Szu Gui San	:	7	Fans
30B	Chuan Dai	:	30	Fans
40B	Shuang Long Bao Ju	:	40	Fans
	Total:	:	84	Fans

Example 5:

1A	Jiang	:	1 Fan
2A	Ping Hu	:	2 Fans
2B	Chueh Yi Men	:	2 Fans
2C	Duan Yiao	:	2 Fans
7K	Szu Gui San	:	7 Fans
60C	Chuan Dai San Shu	:	60 Fans
40B	Shuang Long Bao Ju	:	40 Fans
	Total		: 114 Fans

Example 6:

1A	Jiang	:	1 Fan
2I	Red Dragon Triplet	:	2 Fans
7F	Wu Men Chih	:	7 Fans
7L	Dui Dui Hu	:	7 Fans
	Total		: 17 Fans

Example 7:

2I	Red Dragon Triplet	:	2 Fans
7F	Wu Men Chih	:	7 Fans
7L	Dui Dui Hu	:	7 Fans
30A	San Shu	:	30 Fans
	Total	:	46 Fans

Example 8:

2A	Ping Hu	:	2 Fans
2B	Chueh Yi Men	:	2 Fans
10B	Ching Yiao	:	10 Fans
20B	Shuang Piao	:	20 Fans
	Total	:	34 Fans

Example 9:

2A	Ping Hu	:	2 Fans
40A	Ching Yi Sher	:	40 Fans
40B	Shuang Long Bao Ju	:	40 Fans
	Total	:	82 Fans

Example 10:

2A	Ping Hu	:	2 Fans
2J	Lao Shao	:	2 Fans
7B	San Xiang Fung	:	7 Fans
7C	Huen Dai Yiao	:	7 Fans
	Total	:	18 Fans

Example 11:

1A	Jiang	:	1 Fan
2A	Ping Hu	:	2 Fans
2B	Chueh Yi Men	:	2 Fans
7A	Yi Tiao Long	:	7 Fans
	Total	:	12 Fans

Example 12:

7I	Huen Yi Sher	:	7 Fans
7L	Dui Dui Hu	:	7 Fans
20A	Xiao San Yuan	:	20 Fans
30A	San Shu	:	30 Fans
	Total	:	64 Fans

Example 13:

100B	Jiang Jiang Pung	: 100 Fans
100I	Liang Shu	: 100 Fans
	Total	: 200 Fans

In the Shanghai Game, the number of Fans in a winning hand exceeding 100 but under 200 is not valid. The maximum number of Fans is 200.

The term for 100 Fans is Fung Mun 封門, while that for 200 Fans is Shuang Fung Mun 雙封門.

5.11 Awarding the Winner

As is the case with the Cantonese Game, all players must agree on the rules of awarding the winner prior to the game. If more than one player claims the same discarded tile to complete the winning hand, then the Lower House of the discarder has higher priority over the other players. The Upper House has the lowest priority.

The players can choose *one* of the following ways to pay the winner:

(1)   The discarder pays the winner one full score,

(2)   The discarder pays the winner two times the full score,

(3)   The discarder pays the winner the full score, and the other two players each pay the winner one-half of the full score.

If the Winning Tile is self-drawn, the other three players each pay the winner one full score.

The major difference between the Shanghai Game and the Cantonese Game lies in the award given to the winner. In the Cantonese Game, the award is not linearly proportional to the number of Fans (see Section 2.14). In the Shanghai Game, however, a Fan is a point and a point can be of any value agreed upon by the players. For example, if the total number of Fans is 87, then the full score paid to the winner is simply 87 points.

CHAPTER SIX

THE 12-TILE GAME
十二張

As you gain confidence as a player, you may want to inject more fun and excitement into your mahjong game. One way you can achieve this is to play variations, and a game that offers this is the 12-Tile Game.

The 12-Tile Game is played exactly the same way as the 13-Tile Game except that each player draws 12 tiles instead of 13. Like a wild card in poker, the 13th tile is an invisible (wild) tile, which can be any matching tile a player wishes to designate in his or her winning hand. This greatly increases the possible winning combinations, but also requires great concentration and quick matching skills.

Examples:

(1) If the last three tiles in your hand are No. 1, No. 3, and No. 5 Circle tiles, you will have four winning chances:

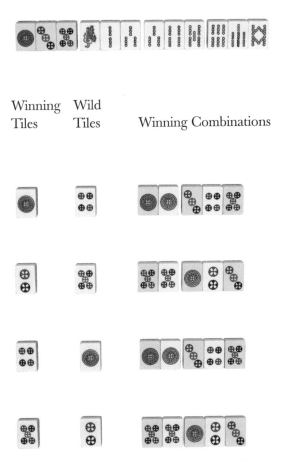

Winning Tiles   Wild Tiles   Winning Combinations

(2) If the last three tiles in your hand are two No. 3s and a No. 6 Circle tiles, you will have six winning chances:

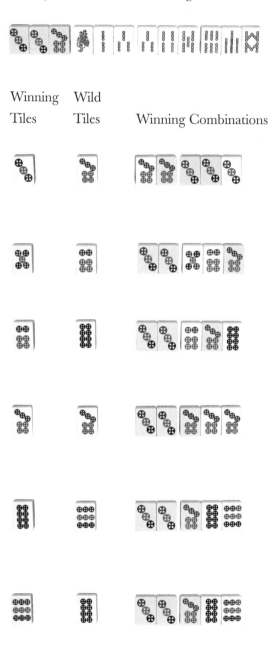

Winning Tiles

Wild Tiles

Winning Combinations

(3) If the last six tiles in your hand are two No. 2s, two No. 3s, No. 4, and No. 5 Circle tiles, you will have six winning chances:

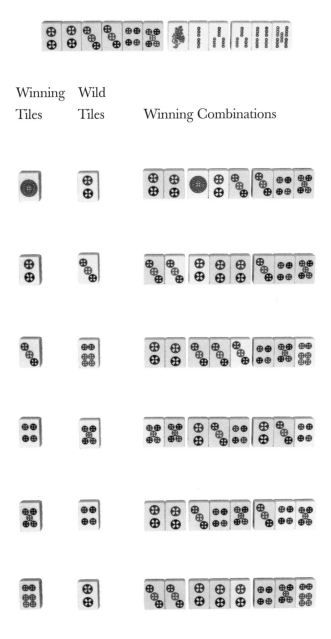

Winning Wild
Tiles   Tiles   Winning Combinations

6.1 Winning Probabilities (The 12-Tile Game)

Ready Hand   Winning Tiles
                                              (any of these numbers)

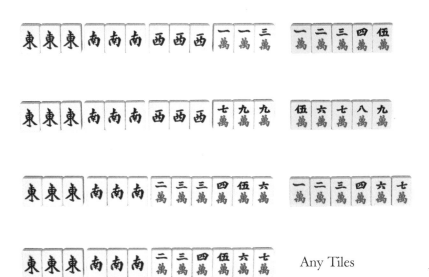

Any Tiles

CHAPTER SEVEN

THE 16-TILE OR TAIWANESE GAME

十六張 臺灣牌

Another variation of the 13-Tile Game is the 16-Tile Game, in which each player draws 16 tiles instead of 13. The game is basically the same as the 13-Tile game but with an extra matched set. Also, the method of scoring and seat allocation is different.

7.1 Seat Allocation (Ban Wei) 搬位

Once the four players have been seated randomly around a square table, one player casts two dice, and the dots are summed. Counting the dice caster as 1, the players are counted counterclockwise until the sum is reached at the position of the chair of the Temporary First Dealer.

Example: If the player at Side A of the table casts the dice and the sum of the dots is two, then Side B is the chair of the Temporary First Dealer. Accordingly, the ruler bearing the Dealer's ensign is placed at Side B.

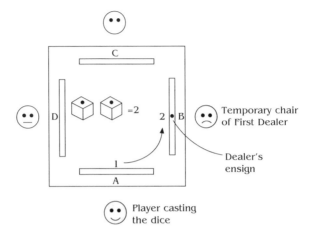

Following this, any player picks out four different Wind tiles, puts them face down on the table, mixes them well, and stacks the tiles in the center of the table.

The player who sits at the Temporary Dealer's chair casts two dice again. Again the dots are summed and the players are counted counterclockwise, with the Temporary Dealer being counted as 1 until the sum is reached. The player who is counted last picks up the top tile from the Wind tile stack. The player on his or her right picks up the second tile, followed by the other players in counterclockwise fashion.

Example: The player sitting at the Temporary Dealer's chair (Side B of the table) casts the dice and the total number is 6. The player at Side C picks up the first tile. Players D, A, and then B, in turn, pick up their tiles.

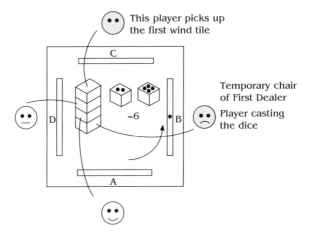

The player who picks up the East Wind tile is the Temporary Dealer and will be seated at the Temporary Dealer's chair (Side B of the table), as determined by the first dice cast. Each of the other players will also be seated at the appropriate seat according to his or her Wind tile.

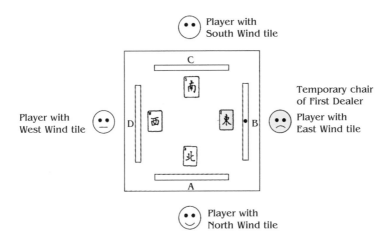

7.2 Building the Walls 整理牌

After all the players have been seated according to their Wind tiles, they all take part in turning the tiles face down, including the 8 Flower tiles, and mixing them thoroughly. Each player then lines up two single rows of 18 tiles each (similar to the Shanghai Game).

7.3 Designating the First Dealer, Breaking the Walls, Revealing Flower Tiles, and Drawing Make-up Tiles 起莊 開牌及補花

The Temporary Dealer casts two dice again and totals the dots. Beginning with the Temporary Dealer, who is counted as 1, the players are counted counterclockwise until the sum is reached. The player who is counted last becomes the First Dealer of the game. The ruler with the Dealer's ensign is, accordingly, placed at his or her side of the table. Next, the wall of tiles on the First Dealer's side is broken. Counting the tiles of this wall from right to left, the First Dealer saves a number of stacks equal to the last sum of the dots on the dice. He or she separates these stacks from the rest and keeps them to the right. The dealer then begins to draw, two pairs at a time. Others follow in a clockwise direction until each player has drawn four times for a total of 16 tiles. The Dealer then draws an additional tile as his or her first draw. After the initial drawing is complete, all the players display the Flower tiles on the table from the initial drawing. Beginning with the First Dealer, each player draws one make-up tile from the end of the wall, for each Flower tile revealed. If the make-up tile happens to be another Flower tile, the player must wait until all the other players have drawn their make-up tiles before he or she can draw another make-up tile. The game can now begin, with the First Dealer discarding a tile.

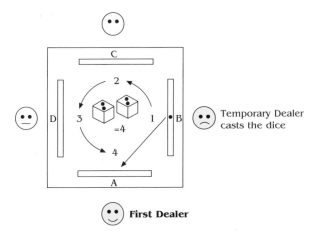

7.4 Shuh 食

When a player claims a discard from his or her Upper House to match a Sequence, the player must place the claimed tile in the middle of the set, face up, in front of him or her.

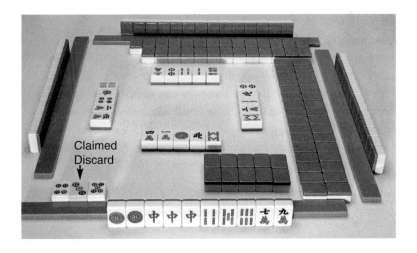

105

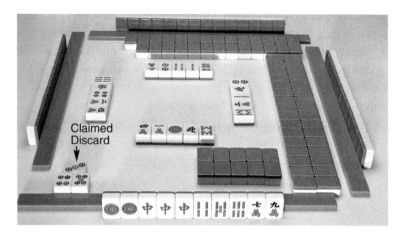

7.5 Garng 槓

When a player declares a concealed Garng or Quadruplet, he or she displays the Quadruplet face down and should not reveal the tiles to the other players.

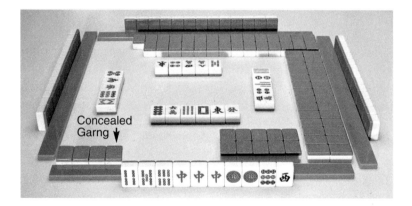

7.6 Winners

A player can complete a hand by drawing the Winning Tile from the walls during his or her turn, or by claiming the Winning Tile when another player discards a tile or declares a revealed Garng. If a player fails to claim the Winning Tile when it is first discarded by a player, however, he or she cannot claim the Winning Tile discarded by other players until after making a discard. Even if the player draws a Winning Tile from the walls, he or she still cannot win until after a discard has been made.

If a discarded tile is claimed by more than one player to complete the hand, there will be more than one winner. Only the discarder pays all the winners.

7.7 Scoring

Scores are counted in terms of Tai (台) instead of Fan (番) and the total score is multiplied by the sum of Tai plus a fixed value called De (底) for the completion of the hand. In general, the value of De is 2 to 4 times that of each Tai.

BONUS TAI

Whenever the Dealer wins, the discarder pays him or her one extra Tai as a bonus. When the Dealer draws the Winning Tile, each of the other players pays the dealer one extra Tai as bonus. When the Dealer discards the Winning Tile, he or she pays one bonus Tai to the winner. When the Dealer repeats as Dealer again, two Tais are added as a bonus for each repetition.

ONE TAI 一台

Hua	花	Each Flower tile earns a Tai.
Wu Hua	無花	Absence of Flower tile.
Tsu	字	Each Triplet of Honor tiles earns a Tai.

Wu Tsu   無字   Absence of Honor tile.

Tsu Mor   自摸   Self-drawn Winning Tile.

Ming Garng   明槓   Each revealed Quadruplet set.

Chiang Garng 搶槓   Robbing a Garng.

Hai Dee   海底   Last tile on the table self-drawn by the winner.

Men Ching   門清   No revealed tile.

TWO TAIS 兩台

An Garng   暗槓   Each concealed Quadruplet set.

Duh Ting   獨聽   The only tile to win, which is a Bridge tile or the tile that matches the eye.

Liang An Kan 兩暗刻   Two concealed Triplets.

THREE TAIS 三台

Wu Tsu Hua   無字花   Absence of both Flower and Honor tiles.

Men Ching   門清不求   Self-drawn Winning Tile of a non-
Bu Chiu   revealed hand.

Xiao Ping Hu 小平糊   All Sequence Hand mixed with either the Flower or Honor tiles (as the eye of the winning hand), or both.

FIVE TAIS 五台

San An Kan   三暗刻   Three concealed Triplets.

Shuh Tsu   十隻   The winning hand is completed when more than 5, but less than 10, discarded tiles are on the table.

Wai Long   外龍   An External Dragon suit, that is, a complete set of numbers, from 1 to 9, of the same suit, found in both concealed and revealed tiles.

Wei Wei   尾尾   Two Triplets plus one pair of Wind tiles.

TEN TAIS 十台

Huen Yi Sher 混一色   Mixed One-Suit Hand.

Dui Dui Hu   對對糊   All Triplets Hand.

Nei Long   內龍   An Internal Dragon suit, that is, a complete set of numbers, from 1 to 9 of the same suit, all found in concealed tiles.

Dar Ping Hu　大平糊　All Sequence Hand with the absence of both the Flower and Honor tiles.

Chuan Chiu Ren 全求人 All Revealed Hand with the Winning Tile self-drawn or claimed.

Ooh Tsu　　五隻　A winning hand completed when only five, or fewer, discarded tiles are on the table.

FIFTEEN TAIS 十五台

Xiao San Yuan 小三元　Junior 3 Chiefs, that is, two Triplets plus one pair of Dragon tiles.

Bao Ting　　報聽　After drawing the 16 tiles from the wall and before drawing or claiming any tile, a player announces that he or she has a Ready Hand and is calling for the Winning Tile. Note: After the announcement, the player may not exchange any tile in the hand or he or she will forfeit the status of Bao Ting.

San Fung　　三風　Three Triplets of Wind tiles.

Szu An Kan　四暗刻　Four concealed Triplets (a Quadruplet is counted as one concealed Triplet).

TWENTY TAIS 二十台

Chi Chiang Yi 七搶一　A player who has seven Flower tiles can claim the eighth flower tile from another player.

THIRTY TAIS 三十台

Bar Tsu Hua　八隻花　Eight Flower tiles.

Xiao Szu Xi　小四喜　Junior 4 Happiness, that is, three Triplets plus one pair of Wind tiles.

Dar San Yuan 大三元　Grand 3 Chiefs, that is, three Triplets of Dragon tiles.

Ni Gu Ni Gu　尼姑尼姑　Seven pairs plus one Triplet (a Quadruplet is counted as two pairs, and must be kept in the playing hand without declaring Garng).

FORTY TAIS 四十台

Dar Szu Xi	大四喜	Grand 4 Happiness, that is, four Triplets of Wind tiles.
Ching Yi Sher	清一色	Pure One-Suit Hand.
Tian Hu	天糊	Heavenly Hand, that is, the Dealer wins on the first draw.
Dee Hu	地糊	Earthly Hand, that is, the Winning Tile is the first discard by the Dealer.
Wu An Kan	五暗刻	Five concealed Triplets. Note: A Garng is also counted as a concealed Triplet.

The Complete Origami Kit
ISBN 0-8048-1816-9   US$14.95 Kit

The Complete Origami Kit for Children
ISBN 0-8048-1973-4   US$14.95 Kit

Origami Extravaganza!
ISBN 0-8048-3242-0   US$22.95 Kit

Deluxe Origami
ISBN 0-8048-3085-1   US$18.95 boxed

Folding Papers for Origami (Large)
ISBN 0-8048-1755-3   US$6.95

Folding Papers for Origami (Small)
ISBN 0-8048-1754-5   US$5.95

Origami: Japanese Paper Folding *by Florence Sakade*
ISBN 0-8048-3308-7   US$10.95

Origami for Beginners *by Florence Temko*
ISBN 0-8048-3313-3   US$4.95

Origami Monsters *by Isamu Asahi*
ISBN 0-8048-3315-X   US$4.95

Origami Greeting Cards *by Isamu Asahi*
ISBN 0-8048-3314-1   US$4.95

Origami Playtime Toy Shop *by Nobuyoshi Enomoto*
ISBN 0-8048-3317-6   US$4.95

Origami Playtime Animals *by Nobuyoshi Enomoto*
ISBN 0-8048-3316-8   US$4.95

Origami Activities for Children *by Chiyo Araki*
ISBN 0-8048-3311-7   US$8.95

ABCs of Origami *by Claude Sarasas*
ISBN 0-8048-3307-9   US$4.95